THE WILD NIGHT DRESS

THE WILD NIGHT DRESS

poems by
LAURA MCCULLOUGH

The University of Arkansas Press
Fayetteville
2017

For Willy and Steven,
my first brothers

At the end of my suffering
there was a door.

—Louise Glück

Everything in the future is a wave,
everything in the past is a particle.

—Lawrence Bragg

All the particles of the world
are in love and looking for lovers.

—Rumi

Series Editor's Preface

Miller Williams was the first editor to spot me, you might say, and subsequently, the one who published my first full-length book of poems, *The Apple That Astonished Paris,* in 1988. With a single stroke, I was transformed into a "published poet," an all-too-common phrase that reminds us of the vast number of poets who are unpublished, or as an optimist might say, "pre-published." Funny, we don't hear much about "unpublished novelists" or "unpublished journalists."

Since then, I have felt a special debt to Miller for the validation he gave me and for the delicacy with which he edited that collection. "You have a line that goes, 'I can see it so clearly.' I don't think you need that intensifier '*so,*'" he told me in our first talk on the phone. I was left with the feeling that this man had read my poems more closely and carefully than I had. I won't forget that initial phone call. Miller happened to find me in a hotel in Miami, where I was getting dressed to go to Hialeah for a day at the races. When I heard him say he was going to publish my book, I knew I'd been granted more than enough luck for one day; it was a pleasure to spend the afternoon losing one race after another. I wasn't just someone who couldn't pick a winner; I was a *published poet* who couldn't pick a winner. The day was made even better because my best pal was with me, and we even ran into Carol Flake, whose horse book, *Tarnished Crown,* was just about to be published.

Judging this prize, which is named in honor of the cofounder and director of the University of Arkansas Press, gives me the opportunity to pass on the gift that Miller Williams gave to me, the publication of a book of poems, in some cases a first book.

For a poet, in terms of sheer thrills, there is no publication that matches his or her first book. With all this in mind, it follows that serving as judge for the Miller Williams Poetry Prize is great pleasure for me.

Even if one is so blissfully egalitarian and nonjudgmental as to believe that all poetry manuscripts are equal, one must concede that some are more equal than others. This year, all of the "more equal" ones were eye-openers for me, literary wake-up calls that brought me to attention, each for a very different reason.

Self-Portrait in a Door-Length Mirror might be an intentional echo of Ashbery's convex mirror, but Stephen Gibson's language is neither coy nor elliptical as Ashbery's typically is. Instead, Gibson presents a series of clear formalist poems, each organized around a different kind of patterning. A series of 8 seven-line poems—each in the rectangular shape of a painting —examines the life and art of Pierre Bonnard. But the focus is Marthe de Méligny, Bonnard's lover, model, and eventually, his wife. The eroticism of Marthe washing her feet in a bathtub or being submerged in it naked is balanced by the mention of the objects in the painting where "everything alive . . . is dead." Add to this grouping an intricately successful pantoum about Diane Arbus, along with my favorite, a twenty-seven-line monorhyme (a tour de force, by the way) written in reaction to a photograph of Hermann Göring's suicide. The radical subjects of Arbus (also a suicide) and SS Commander Göring are brought under control by the imposition of form. The resulting tension shows this exceptional poet at his rhyming best.

Mr. Stevens' Secretary—yes, it's *that* Mr. Stevens—is a series of vignettes taken from (or invented to create) the life of the great modernist's secretary. We see what Stevens looked like from her point of view, which includes how Stevens smelled—not bad as it turns out: "Oriental . . . but that may be that was because of the tea . . . White peony tea." A mild eroticism builds when we are told that the secretary keeps a special bottle of Chantilly "not at home but in her desk." We also get to see the secretary outside of her job in a poem about wasps and marriage and another about her pre-Stevens employers. But it is the famous poet who cannot distinguish *its* from *it's*. In another poem, she attempts to write a fable in which a father saves a cat who got its head stuck in a milk bottle, yet he has an awful temper and shouts "horribly" at his wife. Like Carol Ann Duffy's boldly feminist collection, *The World's Wife*, Frances Schenkkan's *Mr. Stevens' Secretary* forces readers to adjust their perspective by showing a great man through the eyes of a previously silent and less visible woman.

One requirement for poets is the ability to write about two different things at the same time. Seamus Heaney turns writing into a kind of digging. John Ciardi intertwines marriage and the structure of an arch. Among the several poems in Jennifer Givhan's *Protection Spell* that stopped me cold is "The Polar Bear," in which a mother tries to protect her black child from the television news of racial unrest (riots, arrests, brutality) by turning his attention to the Discovery Channel. But there, a polar bear is fighting for survival surrounded by vicious walruses and melting ice. The boy clutches his stuffed white bear and asks if this is real. Life in the Arctic and life in the urban streets are conjoined, ecology and racism wed. Givhan is a poet of great heart and brave directness who writes real-life poems, sometimes crowded to the point of claustrophobia with the details of life in the poor lane. One poem transforms a laundromat woman living "paycheck to paycheck" into a "god." Another poem is a stirring defense of cheerleaders, written without a drop of irony. A reader will be quick to trust the authority in this poet's voice and the credentials of experience that are on full display.

Not all the poems in *The Wild Night Dress* by Laura McCullough use scientific or technological language, but many of them do, and in ways that create interesting effects. This poet has the kind of binocular vision that can see the poetic and scientific aspects of the world simultaneously. The poem "Feed" opens: "In a drone video of Humpbacks / feeding off the coast of Canada, / the surface of the ocean is frothed into blossoms." The ending of that last line returns the poem to poetry's musical origins without implying any friction between this lovely sound and drone technology. In a poem in which the speaker hungers for eggs, this mix of diction occurs: "though I wish to fill myself, / until the ventromedial hypothalamus [the gland that stimulates hunger] / is so stimulated / all I can think of is flowers." This shuffling together of lyrical/botanical and medical language is done so gracefully, it has the effect of bringing "the two cultures" into a rare state of peaceful coexistence. Also engaging are the more traditionally lyric poems, one about childhood, another about a "fawn caught in the family compost" (for me, an echo of the cat caught in a milk bottle in *Mr. Stevens' Secretary*), but the distinction this collection can best claim is the way the poems find an easy synthesis between poetry and science. Perhaps Laura McCullough's most telling confession lies in this couplet: "I can't help loving / the word *sonoluminescence*."

I'm glad that early on, the editors at the press and I agreed that the judge for these prizes should not be looking for poems that sound like the poems of Miller Williams but for poems that Miller might have enjoyed and admired. It's easy for me to picture Miller paging through these four books with a look of appreciation and even delight on his face, though he might keep a red pencil nearby just in case he comes across one of those annoying, unnecessary "intensifiers."

Billy Collins

Acknowledgments

Thanks to Michael Waters, Mihaela Moscaliuc, Timothy Liu, Ray Garman, Peter Murphy, Tara Tomaino, Kathleen Graber, Renee Ashley, Stephen Dunn, Tony Hoagland, and Michael Broek; to the community of writers and artists at the Sierra Nevada Low Residency MFA program, Stockton University's Winter Poetry and Prose Conference, and the Brookdale Humanities Department, all of which I am honored to teach in; to the artists, writers, teachers, and participants of the Virginia Center for the Arts, the Vermont College of Fine Arts Postgraduate Writers' Conference, and the Great Mother New Father Conference; and finally to the editors and publishers of the following who gave homes to poems though sometimes in earlier versions and sometimes before I even knew they could hold their own:

American Poetry Review: "I am calling you" and "Calling it
    Jelly Rather than Jam"

Painted Bride Quarterly Review: "Taking Off the Nightdress"
    (as "Leafless"), "Reclaimed Wood," and "Maggot Therapy

Barrow Street: "Skatterbreak: like balls. like universes" and
    "Everyday Favors"

Boxcar Review: "In Aggregate"

Evansville Review: "The Internet of Things," "Salt and Stars,"
    and "Temple of Sacrifice: Temple of Beauty"

*Forklift, Ohio: A Journal of Poetry, Cooking, & Light Industrial
    Safety*: "There Is Also Up" and "Negatively Charged"

Southern Review: "Searching for the God of Science
    in Broken Glass" and "Angle of Refraction with Dog #1"

Compose: a journal of simply good writing: "Across Which the World"

Michigan Quarterly Review: "Wearing Sunglasses Against the Sun & Smell of Smoke"

Tupelo Quarterly: "Everywhere I Haven't Been Anywhere"

THAT Literary Review: "we all walk from one world to the next"

Hermeneutic Chaos Literary Journal: "In His Sleep He is Gone" and "The ocean was unintentional"

The Great American Lit Mag: "Bodies That Allow"

Meat for Tea: The Valley Review: "Dark Sea of Awareness" and "Walking the highline in the landscape of marginal encounters"

Blue Lyra Press Anthology: "Libretto of Myrrh"

All We Can Hold: A Collection of Poetry on Motherhood: "Hunger Always Returns"

The Good Men Project: "Someone was selling you a pot of failure."

Massachusetts Review: "Feed"

32 Poems: "Passage, Revolving, with Boots"

JuxtaProse: "Dissimulation of Birds"

Harvard Review: "Composition of Body :: Water Glass"

Contents

Part IV: Retreat : Surrender

Coda

PROLOGUE

The Love Particle

The scientist who coined the term *God Particle*
regrets it. It came from his book, *The Goddamn Particle:*

If the Universe is the Answer, What is the Question?
His editor thought it too provocative. The title change

does speak to analogies between science and religion,
both shaping chaos into comprehendible cosmologies

of structures, particles, relationships, time, space,
and the awful rowing towards god and fearful symmetries

poets write of. *Love waves* is the name given to shocks
across the planet's surface after an earthquake, what we

who are not at the epicenter actually feel. Today, a friend
in love asked if she is crazed, should pull back, what

reverberates through her too much to be believed,
trusted, outside of language and sense. During a quake,

solid rock can behave like a liquid, and recently, water
molecules inside beryl, a form of emerald, was found

to face six different directions at the same time, a kind
of *quantum tunneling*, which isn't thought possible

except in another universe. Maybe love is like that?
I tell my friend a new state of matter, *phase transition*

is when we feel the earth roiling like ocean,
and wonder if we will have to grip each other

not to avoid destruction, but to transform

into beings we don't think possible. If we didn't
feel love waves, how would we know?

PART I

PASSAGE WITH HARDBOILED EGG

Feed

In a drone video of Humpbacks
    feeding off the coast of Canada,
the surface of the ocean is frothed into blossoms.
    Whales blow bubbles.
The voiceover explains *toroidal vortexes*

surround fish in a net, herding them
    into a bait ball. I think maybe some
are just for pleasure because as a girl,
    under a tree coming into bloom,
its leaves so translucent

light seemed to rain over me,
    I never felt so alone or so alive.
History is full of bloodshed and acrimony,
    and, like long marriage,
cycles predictably. Maybe

it is no surprise scientists discovered
    a large, interconnected fungus
where the end of one individual blurs
    into where another begins.
Today, at the beach, a shark sighting

thirty feet out; lifeguards whistle fiercely,
    aide-memoire things swim unseen around us.
Once we thought the blue whale

the biggest animal until the found fungus
made us adjust our worldview.

When the lifeguard's whistle cut the air,
     we all thrashed out of the water,
and my husband and I stood
     scanning the surface for fins.
When they let us back in, he stayed

on the wrack line, slim zone
     of skate cases, shells, and Styrofoam;
nothing would lure him back in. Around me
     others were throwing themselves
into the swallowing mouths

of the coming waves,
     to be spit out again.
I kept rising up from the bottom
     as if launching from elemental dark
into elemental light

with pleasure. It's true honey mushrooms
     can become so massive,
their sweet fruiting bodies blossom
     up from the ground
sometimes miles apart from each other.

In the whale video, the singing
        enthralled me, but knowing sound
excites bubbles in liquid, exploding
        bursts of light to blind fish
so they can't escape being eaten

only intellectualizes what I feel.
        I can't help loving
the word *sonoluminescence* and wonder,
        if the fish could get away,
would they even try?

Toward Something Larger

Once I thought I understand systems
but don't; I'm just fascinated, looking up
obsessively for the next falling plane,
then down at the manhole possibly akilter
or an unlatched grate.   There's no winning
when it can come at you from any direction.
If that's all there was,
            this whiplash,
I'd tell you now where my car is parked
and to come get me.   But that's not all there is,
            and to invite
that kind of bad behavior would be an abdication
            of what is necessary
now, a way to feed people, which involves so much
more than satiating the body,

            the body
only an ocean separated from other oceans
            by the merest of membranes,
desperate to be a wave among all these waves,
            connected yet singular
which TV sometimes makes us feel,
before making us feel very afraid.

            I watched TV
from the heel of her bed.   All that grief
in so many places all the time—

and, almost unimaginable in our age of surveillance,
another jetliner
missing.   Someone told me once if you caught
          cancer early,
it was curable.   Maybe what we really mean
          is we can't believe
in a world still so brutal
and barbarous a place.   In pictures
we can see off the southeast coast of Africa,
an illusion of an under-water waterfall,
          submerged cliff,
over which we could be swept down
into the unmapped ocean.

          It took them so long
to say what she knew
          immediately,
telling us, *I give this four months.*

The Center of the Grid

Route 522 was backed up in both directions.
Only those of us at the heads
      of the east and west lanes knew
      a small girl, looking down
      at ice-crusted porch steps
      stepping carefully before
      letting go the last rail,
      oblivious to all of us waiting
      for her to get on the bus,
      was the root
      of our perceived problem.

The day was snapping its fingers—*Don't be late.*
Was there a shadowed face at the front door?
One who would or could not shovel
      that icy walk, treacherous stairs?
The windows were dark.   Was anyone watching
      the child's careful stepping,
      head bent toward
      each ginger boot placement?   But I could feel
      the mounting impatience, exasperation like exhaust
      from all the cars.
We were waiting
      to go to work, the store, hospital.

Finally, she was on the bus, red lights off,
a collective sigh rising through all the metal roofs,
      a measurable suburban relief.   We began
      to go again,   and as I finally passed
under the Garden State Parkway,
      cars rumbling
      overhead on their ways south and north,
      I was suddenly aware
      the four directions
      met right there
      in the winter post dawn light.

Soliloquy with Honey: Time to Die

A box arrived today filled with honeys and a DVD,
Bladerunner, a beautiful violent movie.   In the letter,
my friend chides me for looking away from violence.
He's right, but I wonder whether turning away
is an act of resistance rather than cowardice, but because
I've cared for two people through death, watching
as one's jaw slid down out of its hinge sideways
like a cartoon corpse, does not mean I know anything.
Bladerunner enacts the question of what it means
to be fully human. Replicant Roy Batty, embedded
with memories, gives a monologue, which has entered
the popular lexicon: *I've seen C-beams glitter,* he said,
and, *I've seen things you people wouldn't believe.*
Intelligent, handsome, struggling with emerging emotion,
he is real, yet temporary, despised, though the protagonist
comes to understand Roy is just like us in the end.
I wonder if honeys are like memory—*all these moments*—
                    distilled
from the places they came from. There are five in all
from different countries—including one from Morocco
which I open first, dipping a pinky and tipping it
to my daughter's mouth. *It tastes full of light crystals,*
she exclaims, and I realize I am growing hungry
for what seems to be essentialized only through residues

of bodies that have lived and died,
leaving something
of themselves behind
off which I must learn to feed.

For B.

Across Which the World

What luxury there is in what bees
in Brazil have wept and Turkish beekeepers
have culled from the transformed pollen of flowers
of some German field I can not conjure;   there

in the interstices between neurons across which
both memory and new thought leap, across which

the world is reimagined from what could be
to what is
to what might,

I peer, and think of us, like drones,
and the thrum of this world
that leaves such amazing residue
of what we make together
and of what we weep
into being.

I am Calling You

In the night, I huddled next to her listening
to the tides of her breath   as if a creature
was drowning in a pool,   a winged thing,
unable to dry and lift itself.   My clumsy mammal
hands seemed crude
against her delicacy.   Sometimes I wake
in the night crying: *Mother, are you there?*

In Czech there is a word for getting around paying
for a call, *prozvonit*, meaning *to flash a signal*.

I'm told my parents did this when I was young,
my father in the navy, calling home, then hanging up.

I'm ready to learn another language, a new
syntax.   How desperate this desire to apprehend.

What He Said the Russians Say

How long did I stand on the porch in the cold,
the snow
          sky white, air white, all white in my head

unable to recall the word *mother*,
          a purple spot blossoming behind my eyes,
the door locked,
          tongue of metal not depressing,
pounding, hoping she would hear
and come let me in.

The Scots call losing a word this way a *tartle*.
My father was Scot's Irish Italian and loved
wordplay and aphorism. One of his favorites:
          You know what the Russians say: Toughshitsky.
He would laugh large but also nod, teaching me
how more than one thing can be true
at once, even though I was just a girl
who hadn't yet lost enough to understand
          language
as a door we stand at pondering,

trying to get it open, say what we mean,
and how afraid we are that no one
is even on the other side.

Hunger Always Returns

In the body, the lateral and ventromedial hypothalamus
    balance us—now you are hungry; now you are full—
    yet we know that is not the whole story.
My mother used to say:
    If you only have four dollars,
    spend two on bread for your body
    and two on flowers for your soul.
I didn't understand all the kinds of hunger,
    and that some can never be sated.
Six months before she died,
    she went snorkeling in the South Seas.
Oh, the fish! she told me, and that she'd thrown up
    in the water, perhaps a first sign.   Signs

in language are made of signifiers and the signified.
Mother and daughter are a kind of language.

Today, I hold a hardboiled egg, perfect global signifier;
it was the only food
    my mother made reliably well.
In my hand, this egg; in the mouth of the world:
    Malagasy: *hardboiled atody*
    Spanish: *huevo duro*
    Welsh: *wy hardboiled*
    Burmese: *hardboiled kyaato*
    Icelandic: *harðsoðna egg*

Italian: *uovo sodo*

Romanian: *ou fierte tari*

There are thousands of ways to say this,

        and I'd like to go on, until I can find one

        that satisfies, but I doubt that's possible

        though I wish to fill myself,

        until the ventromedial hypothalamus

        is so stimulated,

        all I can think of is flowers.

Screwdriver Winter

Once Fatima tried to take off the oxygen cannula
when changing my mother,
so she began to sniff, then gasp, pulsox plummeting,
becoming delirious. I fought with Fatima, insisting
she not remove it, and she told me not to tell her
how to do her job.   The next morning
I found the portable oxygen tank left empty overnight,
my mother in a swoon, payback for my intrusion
into Fatima's patient care process.   It was a lesson
inside a lesson, and when I saw her again I talked pleasantly
about her kids, her day, but when she turned her back,
I swiped a screwdriver from her rolling cart, pocketed it,
carrying it like a shiv, fingering
the sharp pragmatism of its tip threatening puncture
against my soft thumb pad, no other use for it
but to remind me of what I could never fix.

Calling it Jelly Rather than Jam

Everything is ceremonial when one of you
is   dying:
buying a scarf
because she loves scarves;   cutting
crusts of bread she can't eat;   calling
not texting, the buttons too small

for her now.   You   love

to remember what it was like   talking
on the phone, listening and   savoring

a particular inflection, turn of phrase,
idiom, and diction, the ceremony
of the mouth
of small things.

Taking Off the Nightdress

In the end, my mother's shoulders,
barely covered and quivering,
were like birds.

        Once, I made a dress
for her, the fabric creamy white, the print
a single brown tree
spanning the width, with stark branches.

It was 1974.   I was fourteen.   Each night,
I taught myself to sew,   feeding
the fabric through the foot,   thinking
how surprised she would be.   I remember

seeing her in it, how we'd both loved the gesture,
minor achievement,
and though it fit poorly, the print
was enough for us.   She wore it once and never again,
let me see her
walk out the door in it.
        Maybe
love's architecture is exposed
when we try and fail at what we mean.

Outside the hospital, winter had flayed everything,
the trees charcoaled against the sky, their shadows
thumb smudges on the institutional snow-hid lawn,

and inside the air
was redolent of shit, flowers, and chlorine.

The first time I changed her clothes, peeling back
from her shoulders
the blue flecked cotton gown,
then sliding a clean pink one up her arms,
we held each other
in the oily light, spent.

Ceremony of a Commonplace
and Unremarkable Moment

Lights refracting in the parking lot's wetness,
        a joy mingled in this waiting, the way cloud
and earth connect, the way the umbrella handle
        feels lucky in my hand, and my daughter's steamy
breath joins the miserable glorious air as if we
        are one respirating body. And so, when the car
pulls in, and the door opens, and a boot emerges
        and touches shining asphalt, and the body lifts out,
raising its own umbrella against falling water
        from the open mouth of the sky, and the body
becomes a moving figure with a bowed head
        coming towards us, the tinkling keys become
                processional
bells with the promise of the ritual opening
        of the door we are waiting by, and I think

for a moment of the panic in me, that, yes, the next
        thing is coming, always about to happen, and then

the person tilting the plane of her face to us
        with a smile, this stranger, who is late today,
is finally here, and we all go in out of the rain.

Passage, Revolving, with Boots

It was the winter all the women wore boots,
a kind of hysteria of uniform:
      brown ones, black ones, beige and tawny,
      with studs and straps, ankle length, knee,
      rows of dangling pairs by clip in all the thrifts—
      we couldn't get enough—flat 80's, Fryes found
      in backs of closets, roll down tops or high over
      thigh, tied with tethers behind the leg or zippers
      on the calves or pull-ons with leather tabs—
all of us clacking down the hospital corridors, heels
wedged or toes pointed,   an army of individuals
so lovely and stylish,
      and it snowed like hell that winter,
            and our leather and suede took a beating,
and I'd watch them, women
who, just like me,
stopped to wipe off
      the crusted black ice
      and ruddy mud,
      stomp small pebbles and broken asphalt
      out of the soles
      as we came
one after another
      after another
            through
the revolving doors.

Revolving Door

There, just inside
    the door whooshing
    its rubber kiss
    against glass
as it goes around
and around, a man is tending
the plants.   He wears blue coveralls;
    his sneakers were once red;
    his eyes meet no one's.

In his hands,
he wields a weapon, cutting leaves.
The falling
    foliage
    not much more
    than a whisper
    we ignore.

Searching for the God of Science
in Broken Glass

I have only helped two people die, and two dogs,
one Barthe, with his three firm, working legs,
the fourth always pinwheeling when we walked—
the joint having healed wrong after a break.
He was so beautiful.

   When I think of the day,
long into loving him, when the pain in Barthe's leg
caused him to open his jaws on my son's face
after a too fast and hard hug
and close them so one tooth indented the brow,
the other just puncturing below the jaw—
though he did not close more than that—
it's the image of us on the floor that haunts me:
the injection sent Barthe's stilled body   where?
His tongue, fulsome muscle of utility and love,
extended longer than I thought possible
onto the linoleum, and I tried to hold it
to prevent this last indignity.

   My other dead
are present for me, as well, in their particulars,
like many cells on the shattered glass art
I saw once on display. It didn't capture light,
but flirted with it aggressively, coalescing
parts in a gorgeous breakage, something better
than the whole it might remember it once was
if glass could have memory.

                    Do I think everything
has memory in the form of energy, so nothing
really dies? I wish I could hold that thought.
My tongue tingles with magnesium depleted nerves,
a mouthful of shards so small they would look lovely
and un-dangerous if I could spit them into my palm

          like the memory of broken beer bottles
I saw on a night street as a child. My mother's
hand was warm around mine, and we walked slowly
in unison, so briefly we were one four-legged animal,
staring at the littered ground in wonder.   Maybe

that's where it began for me, this searching
for beauty in breakage, a way to bear this living.
Mama, I said, *these must be fallen stars.*

PART II

SKATTERBREAK

Water : Waterfall : : Equation : Proportion

I don't speak math, but analogy:
>this is to this
>>as this other thing is to this other thing,
other being the operative word
because everything is always other.   Is it
a trick to insert oneself
into the analogy?   If
soul : spirit :: water : waterfall,
then we are water.   Which no one
would likely object to, nor this resort
to science to justify my assertion
with percentages:
>>The body : 60% :: The world : 70%

Then we might speak of salt,
the percentage of which
in the human body is often used
to argue that we came from ocean.

Ocean : salt :: human : blood
is a theory never proved.   A proof
is simply a body of sufficient evidence,
though even math admits ambiguity.
>   I speak but have no proof, certainly not
a consilience,   just hope,

and some knowledge
that when I expire,   something leaves
my mouth:
        air, water, salt, sound ::

Body a Doorway

It was through her body I came   into being.
Soon she will stop   being
in this way we know being to be.   My brother
stands over us, one hand on her head,
the other on the still fontanel of mine, speaking
for all of us, connecting us   physically
while those who can not be with us are   connecting
                                          virtually.
I have been trying

to make my body a door through which she might pass,
but in these last seconds my mind rebels,
and I barely hold back the small selfish voice: *No, don't go.*

Then it is done.   It is done.
She clenches her jaw and releases her final breath:
the catalyst has burned.   What residue remains,
we can not yet conceive.   All we can do is pick up
our phones, call each other and text,

                            phones buzzing with life.

Negatively Charged

/ my brother used to say
every lake, every body
of water, had a plug,
if only you could find it

that could be pulled, water
emptying / what a thought /
that we might yank a plug
and everything would drain /

it was like that the morning
after our mother died / i couldn't find
the ocean / as if it were gone ::
moving water has negative ions

some scientists say / they say
negative ions promote alpha
waves and increased brain
waves = higher awareness,

better oxygen absorption, and
blood filtering of serotonin
and other contaminants / what
is water / where does it come

from / where does it go /
and what is the relation
of water to waterfall / i could
not understand any of this

even if i were to stand near
the ocean which today I can
no longer find :: i can not sense
the four directions / my brain

is an ocean the plug of which
has been pulled, and going down
is going down in any language
or equation / i have often asked

if rain loves the sky it falls from /
Now i ask, does love sky the rain?

we all walk from one world to the next

you who have had some experience,
you know the valley I mean, and the dark /
how the next day, the ocean was gone, and the sun
somewhere else, the four directions star-collapsed / you
who have had this experience, kiss me, please,
with your warm, moist lips / kisses like blue blazes
on the bark of trees in the woods on the path to water
i can't find / they are lights in this gully,
the only way back
from where i had to leave her
alone in the dark.

Libretto of Myrrh

The last day of my mother's life, I bought
a bottle of myrrh at Dean's market for $4.95.   The main
chemical components of myrrh are:

      a-pinene, cadinene, limonene, cuminaldehyde,
      eugenol, m-cresol, heerabolene, acetic acid,
      formic acid and other sesquiterpenes and acids.

We liked musicals. She took me to see *Jesus Christ Superstar*
at the Papermill Playhouse.
      In the part-dark,
being wooed by community theater, I first
heard those words: *sleep and I shall soothe you, calm you,*
and anoint you, myrrh for your hot forehead, and learned
the concept of libretto,
which is not just the lyrics, but stage direction, too,
the book of the opera
someone has written for the music.

I took her to see *The King and I*
for one of Yul Brenner's last performances,
had saved for a year to buy those tickets.
      We sat silently
together in the audience-dark and watched this re-creation:
a real life woman and man, who were storified, then written into
Anna and the King, a book,
then turned into a musical, then movies,
re-interpretations at every re-iteration, re-enactments

trying not just to get it right, but remake it,
so the art is larger than the lived.

The myrrh was so cheap.   When I performed
being a daughter
whose mother is dying, I was aware of the gaze of the world
and wanted to do it well, but the ending was so predictable.

What I love best about live theater is the end, when the actors
come on stage and bow for our applause, how happy they seem,
how glad we sometimes are for their acting, us standing,
          elbow to elbow, making noise,
them holding hands, too, bowing. Everything in the air
          tingling the rush of another night's success;

then the velvet closes or drops, always red and lush,
absorbing sound,
and we shuffle up the aisles, dispersing
through glass doors.

Skatterbreak: like balls. like universes

I recall the day the pool in our yard collapsed,
80 thousand tons of water released in one moment.
This is a story I have told before,
how us kids were not in the pool, or we might have drowned,
the force of water holding us against the fence
until one wrong inhalation overwhelmed our lungs.
This is not what happened, though
next door, the beagle
perhaps dreaming
of the hunt, of the rabbits he sniffed out
in the tall grasses of the woods behind all our houses,
his paws twitching,
     was suddenly swimming,
     his nose at the chicken wire of the roof of his pen,
     dog-paddling.

We children stood giddy looking at the wrecked yard,
the boys grinning and whispering, *Holy shit,*
and I stared at the neighbor's drenched and trembling dog,
thinking about him trapped in his pen,
asleep one second,
the next, swimming for his life.

The Business of Feeding People #1

The people still living need to be fed;
they are up there, pounding feet across wood floors, waiting
to eat again, as soon as I can carry
these dead legs up the long stairs. In another time or culture,
I'd be wearing black, or there would be a wreath on the front door
warning people my mind
is slipping between worlds, no refuge
anywhere,   which is why for now, I just stay here
in the basement
folding laundry, thinking
how my mother rolled her towels, and because clothes
are in un-separated hills on this old wooden table,
at least my bumbling is hidden a while from others.
          For now, I am trying
to get things done, handle business as usual, but in an unusual way—
make bills, pay meals—yet there is nothing in the fridge,
and I don't know where the checks are kept.   Nothing
about this makes sense.
          You can't make bread out of rocks,
          fill bird feeders with confetti,
          but everything gets done in some fashion,
          and the fashion, in some ways, doesn't matter.
          No one
is here
to judge me but me, grown woman
without a mother; I tell myself
Whatever you do now, you are free to do.

Upstairs, their mouths are gaping
like birds, their own sorrows swallowed for years ahead.
I will try not to feed them my own, instead will give them
boards;   it's time they learn
how to hold a knife.

Everywhere I Haven't Been Anywhere

Repudiate felt good in my mouth,
like someone else's tongue.

STEPHEN DUNN

Stephen says—though I'm sure someone else did first—
if a person hasn't found out who they are by forty, they're doomed,
but what is a person but an illusive, allusive island
the coordinates of which
change depending upon the decade, the tides, climate upheaval,
sinking this year into the depths just to rise
again the next in another part of the world.   The world
doesn't know who it is, and it's old, should have its shit together,
and I don't hear anyone just writing it off. Well, actually, I do
all the time, but think they're fools, not for finding fault
or wanting to fix things, but for not having hope.   Today,
I rolled down my car window in the parking lot of Lowes
and asked the guy next to me, *Hey, how's your soul?*
Just fine, he said and paused, *My conscience is clear.*
I said I'd never thought about the connection
between conscience and soul. He said, *You're welcome to the insight.*
Inside, I bought some two dollar, ninety-nine cents succulents
from the coast of Africa and Madagascar, and later planted them
in a shallow bowl. They don't need much root room,
can grow against gravel, live without water; all they need
is light and someone who cares enough to move their bowl
around now and again to catch the beam of the always

shifting sun. I'm told that eventually, unpredictably,
    the split
rock succulent will open as if it has a mouth
out of which a small strange flower
will emerge.

"Someone was selling you a pot of failure."

The day my husband left, I bought six succulents
　　and planted them in tiny pots, happy with their fullness,
their little windows to let light in at the ends
　　of their bubbly leaves looking like fat toes or thumbs.
Google shows me pictures of Madagascar,
　　　　that island romanticized for its vanilla and four-syllabled
　　　　　　name,
　　　　rocky coast colonized by villages of the tiny specimens
　　　　arranged in pebble-filled bowls on my table in Little Silver
　　　　on the east coast of a continent I have never traveled across
　　　　except by air, which is how these came to me,　　and because
　　　　someone knew me and my whole consumer clan
　　　　of buying-frenzied folk so well, they knew I would pay
　　　　four bucks a piece for these adorable exotic, miniature
　　　　cutie-pie plants,
　　yes, because　　　　　　they understood me and my needs,
　　　　and they needed the money,　　　　and someone
　　　　on the island of M. made a few pennies for collecting them,
　　　　and I peer down at them now surrounding my laptop,
　　　　my sorrow seeping into those little green windowed leaf-tips
　　　　in a mock-photosynthesis, and smile though I have read
　　　　the post, which is the title for this poem,
　　　　because I bought them—was *sold* them—without knowing

what to do,　　　how to care for them,　　keep them alive,
in fact how　　　not to kill them,　　and realize
they will die here,　　with me,　　in this house;

it's only a matter of time.

46

The "Internet of things" (IoT) is becoming
an increasingly growing topic of conversation
both in the workplace and outside of it.

Easier to speak of things, how they connect
or don't, and hope—because what else is there?—
for a new economy because our children are indebted
worse than us, and we are full of debt, constipated
on our diet of things /
that make us feel something when we are unsure
about anything anymore /

because we folded the meta-narratives into origami
boats, floating thousands of them like ducks on the sea
of our lost cultures /
and they got soggy and matted together
filling the gullets of sea birds and seals
who washed up dead
on the shores of our imaginations /

    because
we can't really contain that horror, not sure what
is a media scam, skyped-hype, looping distraction /

    or
what to do about it anyway: didn't someone say making
a thousand paper boats was a ritual?   A prayer?
Or was that cranes?   And should they have been hung
on trees?   Easier, yes, to speak of the Internet of Things,

the virtual *now* shifting the paradigmatic architecture
of the real, except /
we're still alone,
like an opportunistic sea gull who can't be blamed
for eating cigarette filters and tampon wrappers,
and so dies,
becoming carrion for other marine life,
its fellow sea birds.

Salt and Stars

You will know the wrack line and how to walk it,
    and that lovers and spouses go alone sometimes,
bringing back small gifts from separate journeys:
    eel grass, skate cases, a loggerhead turtle shell,
a whirled splinter of driftwood, one of the plastic
    baby ducks that circled the world: *look my darling,*
I brought this home for you to the alter of our life.

Isn't this how we live? How we go on when the tides
    of life take us one way, then the other, washing us out
into the many griefs—losing a job, a spouse, a parent—
    and then back again into the warm shallows that renew—
new friendships, other joys we didn't know were possible
    and then suddenly do, and the living becomes good again?

And often, you will walk the line together, arm in arm,
as you do now,
the water on one side, the immensity of ocean reminding you
not that we are insignificant,
but that we are each bodies of water as well,
and full of wonder,

and the land will remind you to be grounded and courageous
through the storms that will come,
because there will always be an accidental tide pool
filled and still like a mirror reflecting back the first evening stars,

or the taste of sea salt on the skin
when one of you has come back from a swim,
or the light growing as the moon rises to help you walk home
together
when it's getting dark.

For M & W

Lowes, capitalist system of instantaneous gratification that never gratifies, you evil bastard, you

They promised next day delivery for the new stove,
so we stayed up all night ripping and tearing, reworking
the electric, pulling out the 50s appliance weighing
twice as much as me, but then they never showed,
so we called, and they said, *Gonna be a few days*,
and we bitched and moaned,
and they said, *Okay tomorrow*, and then we ordered Italian.
Then tomorrow came, and they called
and said, *There's damage to the order*,
so they had to send it back to the warehouse
and did we want another one? *Yes*, but Jimbo—that was his name—
said it was too late for next day delivery,
at least he thought so—and he was new
and his boss had gone home sick—and Jimbo'd
have to call us back later when he figured out what was going on—
it was only his first job and he just wasn't sure—
and we said, *Okay*, and then ordered Thai.
When we didn't hear back, I offered to call and make some noise,
which shamed my husband, so he called back, but Celeste
said Jimbo had gone home sick, too, and no one was around,
and she had no idea, *Sorry. Sorry*? I heard my husband say,
*Me, too. I gotta feed my family, and now
I'm out a stove a third night in a row.*

Silence. He looked at me mugging a face that read,
What can I do? This new kid on the phone hasn't a clue either,

which bummed me out, in fact, I was getting mad,
and he put the phone down and said, *Look out the window,*
and I did. *See the hummingbird?* which I did,
feeding from the honeysuckle manic on the trellis. We

watched a second. Saw it dip its long beak in
and out of the flower goblet. *That hummingbird's name
is Olaf,* I said, *He called out from work today and is drunk
on nectar.* My husband was hoping to be let off the hook
for not yelling at Celeste. The hummingbird disappeared
in a flight of broken dashes my eye couldn't follow.
I looked at my husband. He was smiling, glad I was letting go
the stress. I looked back in the yard trying to see
where the hummingbird went,
imagined catching it,
squeezing it tight in my fist.
Let's order Cuban, I said.

Temple of Sacrifice : Temple of Beauty

The morning the ocean was gone,
I stood on solid ground
only to feel it loosen beneath me—like pleasure
when water charging in cold around your feet
carves out a well beneath you, and you sink,
ankles first, then almost to the calves before
you can't stand the cold anymore and pull out
and step back
(as if it's possible to move away from the incoming tide)—

but there was no ocean, so it was not a pleasure,
and when I turned to look at the land behind me
where I stood on the wrack, I saw it was gone, too,
and all there was was this strip of—not liminal—
but ground of confluence,
the opposite of sacred, instead a junk yard
of the broken and washed-up, which included me,

and my legs seemed to unbuckle from my hips,
and my arms drifted off as if some internal plastic band
had finally eroded, given way, my headtilting, eyes closing on
               their lights,
bobbling off into the air like party balloons
to pollute some distant place,

some parts of me going toward the temple
that had been the sea,
some to the temple
that had been the land,
whatever hollows where I'd once stood gone
because even the wrack line
had been just an illusion.

PART III

SYNTACTICAL
NATURE

Route 35 not far from Colts Neck

Horse flag flips in the too warm air, sun set
      to autumn, but a hot snap bringing everyone's brains
to just below boil. Even the person stopped in the car next to me
      is holding her head. *Hurts?* I ask out my window,
and she says, *I thought it was just me.*
      I pull up
when my lane allows, and the woman with the headache
      still has her hand on her head back there, waiting
for the van to move, but for a minute, out
      my passenger window, I can see the sentient eyes
as big as tea saucers, one, then two, and can only
      imagine their bodies inside there, the way they must
balance as the van rolls through traffic, along
      these human-made asphalt pathways, crisscrossing
the world, or how they feel about the speed
      they don't generate themselves, their hooves flat
against metal, and then my lane moves again, and I
      press my foot to the pedal that makes the gas push
into the chamber that makes this engine go, gather
      momentum, leaving everything behind, as if this is
possible, as if I might escape whatever is chasing me,
      and some invisible force whips against my neck,
the hair lifting, so for a second, I feel an animal
      self, and then turn a corner, and I am home.

Dark Sea of Awareness

From my spot
hunkered on the couch by an open window,
I see the old woman next door carted out
for a walk by the live-in nurse.

Last month, I saw the nurse walking along
Willow Ave. in the rain, and I stopped,
offered her a ride.   I didn't ask about her job—
caring for my neighbor, Maisie—

just about her, and she seemed pleased enough
to share.   She sees me now, and waves one hand,
the other holding the handle of the wheelchair,
her neck bent to keep the phone between ear
and shoulder from dropping on the asphalt,

and her one scrunched eye connects with me,
or maybe not, but she does wave,
and Maisie—her hair whiter and wilder
than I'd seen it before—is bent forward
in her chair, hands like sticks in her lap.

I want to call out, but can't remember
the nurse's name or whether I ever knew it at all.

Mystery and Frequency

When I fell in love ten years into my first marriage,
my lover sent me a link for (Le Mystere des Voix Bulgares)
the Bulgarian women's choir we've now heard
in so many commercials and Tarantino films. My mother
had just discovered Ladysmith Black Mambazo,
and it's easy to forget that Ladysmith is generally peopled
by male vocalists, Le Mystere by females,
and though both wear traditional cultural costume,
their harmonies transcend gender, both
affecting the nervous system, aligning energies. The ocean
bio-acoustician Michael Stocker might call them
cooperative acoustical communities, and the audience, including
my mother and me, respectively, resonating
to the world in our own ways, were connected across vastness
of generational iconic landscapes, but also through
the porous veil I keen through. *Where have you gone?* I sang;
I sang not alone, my family, too, singing with me
as I stood at her memorial, others rising from hard seats,
hands held to air—*where have you gone?*
Respirating in the ocean of air, thrumming insects
or cetaceans; do all beings recognize this loss?
Find respite in the choraling? Crickets sound to know communal
size. Bombs, even when they don't kill, disrupt
Gaza, brains dancing without joined rhythms in so many skulls.
The world is full of men and women who once

were *Other*, exotic, and bouncing the centralized human
into cis-self: we are not all one until we noise
together, this *becoming* something dissident and directional,
the way out opening like a silent water door
through which we might safely swim.

Walking the Highline in the Landscape of Marginal Encounters

Rails to trails are the epitome
     of upcycle, repurpose, tracks
kept and plants planted, art installed,
     and moving now people,
instead of trains, under their own
     steam, a joyful breathiness
in the breeze off the Hudson,
     but also in the faces, as if here,
above things, in the soft air
     beneath the well tended trees
and upscale architecture overhanging
     it (you can see
a midcentury recliner behind the lit
     glass wall there to the left)
we all felt our spines loosen, faces
     nearly happy, yes, plenty
of tourists, but not only, and everyone
     just shy of a little laughter,
and when at one end, my children
     wanted snow cones from the vendor,
at 5 bucks a pop, that early August
     late afternoon, how could I refuse?
We, pleasantly tired from strolling,
     watched him assemble them,
squirt raspberry slush into a plastic
     flower bowl, then crushed ice—

pack it down—squirt some more—
        ice it again, his plastic sheathed
palming of the growing ball
        condensing it—more slurry across the top—
this cycle went on until the first
        child's summer snowball was done
and handed to her with the elegant
        bow only someone accustomed
to the public can manage with dignity
        and then a red spoon and straw
dipped into it at the last moment
        with a flourish. What showmanship!
He was pleased we were pleased
        at what pleasure he could render. Then,
Uh, oh, he said, *a fly.*
        I turned, didn't see it.
Oh, no, he said, to my quizzical
        look, *Some days they follow me home.*
So sweet? I averred.
        He laughed, *Oh yes! Sometimes*
I change my clothes four times
        a day, but still, I am covered
in sweet by dusk. His face was brown
        and broad and freckled, his teeth
white like sugar cubes. Finished now
        with the second snowball—

coconut for my son—he did his bow
and came low to hand it off.
We locked eyes and both grinned.
When I gave him a twenty,
and he rummaged for change, I waved it off.
What a day we've had, I said.
Thank you, he said.
When my daughter spooned a cold mouthful
to my face, I opened wide. It was delicious.
More, I said, meaning *everything*.

The Syntactical Nature of Reality

I.

At the Starbucks in Red Bank today, a long line snaking
around to the counter, everyone shifting their weight
from one side to the other in a crazy jazz pattern:
the guy in the lederhosen slouching his hip
toward the sandwich case; the girl in Lululemon pants
kicking one foot out now and then toward the door;
the woman with the long gray hair clutching the newspaper
tipping up and down on her toes. All with an order
if they are like me, they're repeating
obsessively in their heads—
café mocha with only two pumps chocolate, low fat, no whip—
trying hard not to forget what it is they really want.

2.

Let's meet behind the bakery where the trash cans
smell of burnt sugar and powdered cinnamon,
where Jacko, the homeless guy the local kids
always make fun of, goes to drink from discarded cups
and eat pizza crusts and old donuts.
He has such a good beard.
If you meet me between the two dumpsters
maybe we can work out that problem
we had last week in the meeting,
or should I say *conflict*,

or was it a *communication glitch*?
Did we bobble the snap of our delivery?
but now I've gone into football,
which is where I know you'd rather be
on a Sunday like this one.   Okay, stay home.
But I'm going down there alone.
To that bakery.   I like it best
when it's closed.

3.

Self-reliant like a cat, I feed myself
kale chips and hardboiled eggs
on the train from Secaucus to Mahwah.   This business
of feeding people never ends.   For a long time,
I was hungry.   Now the
                                             lightness
in my belly
makes me hear people better, and the older
I get, the easier it is to allow things to pass
into my ears and then out again, like fat
melting away, my urine full of minerals and proteins
as it cleans out what is left

                              after the body
                              takes what it needs.

Everyday Favors

I sounded out a hope
the alarm clock sounding
the ritual again of work and love
that nearly kills love   nearly
will we do for breakfast today, love,
children's lunches, the thermos,
the mismatched and bent spoons
that never quite closes anymore
        unless we push

a hope I threaded through
sounding time to do
love of work
nearly and what
the damned happy
its lid cracked,
in the drawer
unless we push,
really hard.

PART V
RETREAT : SURRENDER

In His Sleep   *He is Gone*

Gone into sleep where no one can call him
back, steal the French fries off his plate,
ask for help doing all the things
they won't or can't do for themselves, even

me, as I touch his shoulder and hip bone
hoping to alter his night
breathing, feel him rise back
to me, back here, do that thing
that always helps
me sleep, but on his hip

I feel the mountain he

is walking on, and his shoulder is mossy
with places he longs to go,

                                    so I curl away,
close this
door, listen
to the wind threading my lungs,
in a wilderness of hills I don't know
yet how to claim.

Composition of Body :: Water Glass

The body is made
of elements, and we   are mostly water,
but by elemental mass, we're really   oxygen.
Oxygen is the most abundant   molecule.

I am a molecule, bombarded by other   molecules
colliding   continuously   and because we—
all of us as molecules in the vast ocean   of reality—

have different velocities, we pelter,   helter skelter
which is random though less random   than it sounds,
and has a name, Brownian Motion,   the zig sagging

and ricocheting part of the rippling   we sense across
the surfaces of all of our own water,   and because we are
bodies of water submerged   in bodies of water,

today, I woke near drowning and knew
        if I opened my mouth, the song that would leave
                would be both of science and sorrow, and what

would enter would be you. You all, the Other
        and the *other* and the *other*, meaning, when
                I finally opened my eyes, I would have a kind

of multi-bridity of sight: multiple-hybridity,
        the only surrender possible for me in my glass
                of water trembling on the edge of a universe

we made together. In this way,   I might float.

Lake of Sky: Refrain

my mother died Saturday night.　　how do i say that?
before her
death, i prepared myself for being
a doorway.　　i brought her favorite book
The Best Loved Poems of the American People,
a battery operated candle :
a scarf i have that is a prayer
shawl, a tallit, white, with strange long strands
of twisted thread.　　i brought myrrh in a small bottle.
wore a necklace Suzanne gave me of a metal silver sun.
read her favorite poems : made an alter with the candle
and books : anointed her feet, hands, forehead, kissed
the mouth that had once kissed me and whispered,
Oh my baby girl, but now had been open all day like a geode,
dentures twinkling in the lights,　　moisture drying
like a pond out of season,　　only the moving air
in the cannula sounding　　its echo of wind,
her face going white　　like a reflected cloud.

What I hold now as the sun　　is her face inside of mine,
and when I kiss my brother,　　I hear my own voice
whispering:　　*I will kiss you*　　*like she would kiss you.*

Angle of Refraction with Dog

Once on a night street from my childhood
in Jersey City, I knelt to touch glass, saying,
Mama, these must be fallen stars.

Her hand warm around mine, we were one
four-legged animal, staring at the littered ground
with dual wonder. That might be where it began
for me, the searching for a god of science, a way
to bear the accidents of beauty and love.
And when I think of the day, long into loving him,
pain in my dog Barthe's leg caused him to open
his jaws, so only one tooth indented my son's brow,
the other just puncturing below the jaw, I think
of holding Barthe's the injection sent him—where?
        I carried a shard of that glass
home, placing it under my pillow
hoping God would take it back to the sky.
My mother let me believe this, removing it
herself, I am sure, before morning,
first grace and also a lie.

Between Mule Deer and Crow

I.

The mule deer on my path has ears long
as my forearm. She could have moved away
long before I saw her, but stayed.
Is she curious about me?   Nothing
in her eyes betrays this. My scientist friend
would admonish me not to anthropomorphize,
but I admire her seeming self-possession and silence.
The crows have been all chatter, fluttering nearby.
Perhaps they wish to warn me about something.
My phone pings a Google Alert: something
else is happening in Gaza.   Something is happening
everywhere.   Above me, four crows
tussle, hopping twig to branch in unison
as if they are tethered
together at the legs.

2.

My daughter's left hand is the mule deer of the west.
Her right, the deer of the east coast suburbs, lithe,
secretive, stealing hostas by night.   Her left
has ears long as my forearm, and meat on bone
with weight.   Between her hands is a country
I have crossed by air but now must walk if I am
to understand it.   To know what lurks
in the underbrush.   What beautiful
frightened thing is biding its time.

Reclaimed Wood

Now I have begun to henna
　　　　my red hair gone dull
in parts and penny bright in others.
　　　　　　I'd always tried to subdue
its ferality, but when the hull of our
　　　　marriage busted rock

and began to leak, we both thought
　　　　　　it was a good idea to renovate
the kitchen, together, by ourselves.
　　　　　　We closed up the hall
to the back rooms to create more
　　　　　　privacy and took down a load-

bearing wall in hopes of opening
　　　　　　the "flow." My husband looked
like Christ hauling the salvaged
　　　　　　timbers from a warehouse deep
in the Jersey woods one by one
　　　　　　up the front stoop, laying

them in our suburban living room,
　　　　　　posing as a Brooklyn loft.
We framed the new wide space:
　　　　　　one as header, two as column braces,

then sat on the floor cross-legged
      looking at our work in progress,

the way the wood had aged,
      the colors and striations, notches
and hammered pegs. We felt our
      fifties ranch had a new story now,
something with weight, and we
      held hands a little while before

getting up, heading to the shower,
      falling back into our routine. And
me, copper hair frizzing about my head,
      thinking, *What can go wrong?*

Wearing Sunglasses
Against the Sun & Smell of Smoke

Four boys I don't know arguing in the public pool
asked me to arbitrate.   I'd been looking toward them,
but was lost in my grief and wearing sunglasses. *No,*
I said, *I didn't see anything.*   It was clear they were
                surprised,
a clue they were used to well-intentioned adult supervision.
                Why not try talking this out yourselves?
They did.   Shook hands.   I said, *I'm proud of you*
to the boy who still looked peeved I had abdicated some job
he thought I had by nature of my age.   What disappointments
he has ahead.   As my mother lay dying, she confessed
in the night she didn't believe anyone really loved her.   *Why*
are you even here? she'd asked.   My obvious answer
bringing tides of confusion across her loose face.   *But*
why *do you love me?* Her blue eyes, seemingly paler
each day, glowed in her face with puzzlement and need.
Those boys broke apart after the conflict was resolved
and took to different ends of the pool.   I stopped watching.
                The sun overhead was harsh
in a saturated blue sky, almost impossible to look up into.
                The smell of burning underbrush was in the air.
I didn't know if it was from a controlled burn or a lightning
strike.
                No one around me seemed to care.

Bodies that Allow

When she began to fall in the hospital bathroom
after faking sleep for hours until she thought
she could drag herself out of bed
without waking me, I heard her moan.
It wasn't of pain or fear,
but even as I flung myself upright
in the hinged recliner tossing my legs over
the hard plastic arm, I knew
what underlay that sound.
                I opened the door,
and she began to slide against the wall.
                Without knowing what to do, I did
what I knew to do: my arms shot
into the spaces under hers, catching her in my elbows,
which wasn't enough, and we sunk
to the floor, her full weight having let go,
and I pulled her to my chest and let my knees bend,
so she wouldn't hit the wall, the toilet.

The nurse Bernice and I cleaned her
together after I carried my mother to bed
and laid her down gently as I could, which I know
wasn't gentle because I am not very strong,
and I tried squeeze the tears back, my face crumpling
as my mother whispered, *Oh, I am so ashamed,*

but she'd never seemed more
beautiful, flesh creamy and soft,
a body you would want
to hold
in the night, lovely and generous.

In Aggregate

The teenage cashier asks about the swallow tattoo
on my arm as I pay him.   I don't tell him my mother
has just died, and it's for her.   When he turns
to get a bag, I see the peacock on his shoulder
emerging from his muscle-T.   Twenty of my swallow
would fit inside it.   *Did you hear*
     about the boys in Gaza this morning? I ask.
It's stupid of me, insensitive, but I am only half human today.
Where? He asks.   His eyes are thoughtful,
     dark, the brows full black, with stray hairs in the middle.
His jaw is still young, won't finish widening for years yet.
     How can I speak?   *Is the honey really local?* I ask.
Grinning, he shakes his head *no, no*, side to side,
     but says, *Yes, sure is.*
I look at a bin of roma tomatoes
     then up toward the hilly horizon, yellow
     with a grass I can't name, and hear a sob,
and know it's from me,
my face muscle composure collapsing
for a moment.
     How can I tell him
it is the ripeness,
the taut arc of skin on these fruits
picked by someone I don't know,
or that I won't walk on these hills I am driving through
or that I wonder how many men laid this asphalt

we stand on that smokes in this hotter than normal day,
and that I know the cracks are shovel-filled at night
anonymously by public works workers here, as everywhere?

Who has laid these white lines in the parking lot? I want to ask.
Who filled this jar
      of honey now in my hand?   My face recomposes,
so I am no longer a monster.   Or at least no longer look like one.
I pay five dollars for what would,
      back home, at Sickles Market,
      cost nine.
He holds out the change, and I graze
my knuckles along his palm.

The ocean was unintentional. It did not hate

me or even consider me at all.   Before it, I could
not go east.   I'd come from the west again
and again to this point, unable to go further, afraid
of boats, mistrustful but curious
about what is below, swimming a kind of posing,
intoxicating to touch the mystery with so little at stake.

But here I stand.   I don't care about my past.

South, the sun crooks a finger—*this way, this way.*
North is safer, saner: I can see comprehendible lights.

Once, I might have made a choice between these two
directions. Now, I stand into the holes being scooped
out below me in increments;   I had no idea of this until
my balance was endangered.   Like a dumb land
mammal, I keep hauling one flat foot up to replant it,
over and over, scanning the air for a sign
of what I can't perceive with my gross senses,
something transcending what I know about physics
and space, time and intention, water from air, borders
between, spaces we pass over, as if space was something
we understood, as if we were solid, and not full of air
and water ourselves.

There is Also Up

Someone said we live at the bottom of the air,
    that we are the bottom feeders of atmosphere.

We swim in gasses, not liquids, and call it ambulating.

Maybe this is one reason we fly, yet even those of us
    who love the un-kiss of wheel from world,
    aren't we sometimes a bit fearful in the exhilaration,

    a bottom note we can't do without? Is anyone not ever afraid?

You, the one there thinking up means of self-
destruction, can I hold your hand?   Look at me;
look me right in my better eye.   Do I see your sorrow?

Rage?   And the fear of sorrow and rage?   Let me see it,
please?   A small, winged creature in the dark.
It is part of your beauty,
your being, and this swimming
is the way we sustain each other.

For T.

>Retreat: ocean : air : diamond: surrender<

    I.   It surges forward. It bearsdown.
Rises up, creeping. Presses in.

   II.   Diamonds are made in some version
of this: compression. Start with
carbon dioxide, what we exhale.
Burn and squeeze—two kinds of
pressure—then face toward the
surface of the world.

  III.   The ocean at the edge of the wrack.
In winter when ice is all there is.

  IV.   Synthetic diamonds are essentially
the same minus slavery.

   V.   Better than surrender.

  VI.   Re enter. Re engage. What is it?

Buffet

Girl with a new bathing suit asks,
Will I bleed every day for the rest of my life?
 How can I tell
her the truth, which is
the bleeding has barely begun.
We eat.
Me: little.
Her: eggs, waffles, bacon, cereal, yoghurt,
 sausage, kiwi, milk, tea, and chocolate cake.
More. Everything, as it should be.
Me: there is a bowl of blackberries.
I stare at it a long time.
At her, eating.
At the bowl, brimming.
One berry: its seed head like a dreamed multi-verse.
I turn it with a fingernail. Letting morning light caress it.

She leans forward with her bright mouth open.
 Her eyes closed,
Still believes in this world.

The Business of Feeding People #2

The morning
my love told me his love had grown larger
than our house and that no walls could contain it,   he
was afraid I would close the windows and
doors,
but there is no keeping the universe
out
or anything in.

My hand trembles holding
a glass of water overfilled,

Sometimes we feel trapped in this family we've made,
the needs so many,
various, insistent, and urgent, always.
In his hands,
I once saw the universe was larger than
where this shore
meets this ocean. Now, he may leave.
Perhaps I will
never leave this wrack line,
where my self has collected into being, yet
I'll try
to honor the enormity it all is.
So much time has passed
since that plane went down off the coast
of Malaysia,

and is still unfound, a mystery receding
into the mysteries we resign ourselves to.

the meniscus to the lip,
its concave

When the water rose here once, it came
in one of the ways water does,
a revelation
of savagery
rendering everything else insignificant.
We were
naturally afraid.
It did not feel cleansing; it felt like death.
That it did
go back is a kind of mercy, and still
everyone
was hungry, needing to be fed,
but nothing
seemed or seems to ever fill the emptiness.

Nearby the ocean is calm,   and I wonder
about the ways we harm each other
quietly, with no sense
we are doing so.

like a jugular notch in
which I might drown.

A Thousand Acres of Whale-thought

The beginning of love is a horror of emptiness.

ROBERT BLY

The news the morning I decided to opt out of dreaming
    was about a young man's scheme
    to help the ocean clean itself.
He'd crowdsourced his idea, raised enough on Kickstarter
    for the first wave of his plan: a 6,500 foot plastics collector
    off the coast of Japan. As opposed to nets,
    his invention would allow whales and dolphins to swim
    underneath unharmed.
Someone told me, in Chinese, the nature of a question means
    it is a problem
    requiring action and solution,
    thereby insisting on a relationship of obligation
    in the mere utterance.   I was busy thinking
    about someone else's petition for his release from the dream,
    whether that's a relinquishment of obligation
    or the fulfillment of one,

    and of my own love of drama,
    whether it is necessary any longer
    since it didn't seem to solve
    anything, in fact, seemed to feed it,
    like microplastics, which can't be caught by anything,
    so small, they are emulsified, ubiquitous, un-strainable,

and so enter the mouths of large creatures whose job it is
to let everything pass through them.   My friend

said he wished he could understand
Cantonese but can only read it, let it in through his eyes
instead of his ears.   I wish I could understand
the nature of leaving.

Someone is always going away, changing the weather and tides.
When I was a girl, we built pebble and stick dams along the curb
        to hold back the rushing water after a rain.
An emptying pool had us all on our knees,
        hands cupped with crushed rock scooped
        from gravel driveways.

I donated twenty dollars toward hope,
        though my view of water is not the same:
        what you can't see is still dangerous.

A man told me he could tell what bottled
        water brand he was drinking just by taste.
Said he won five hundred dollars once on a bet.
I've never understood the nature of risk.
        Or the delight some people get from it.
I might swim into the wide open mouth of this life
        if I wasn't so afraid of being swallowed.

Maggot Therapy

Near death, sometimes the hands curve
        into themselves like claws.
I held my mother's open, smoothing
        the fingers, trimming the ferine nails.

Once, years before, my husband and I awoke
        to a fawn caught in the family compost,
a hole on its back end festering with worms,
        and he pinched each one out

swiping his little finger in the bowl
        of the wound, then coating it
with antibiotic salve. I loved him,
        and how he saved this small thing.

It's a story I have told over and over.
        Today though, I'm thinking of the medical uses
for maggots: biodebridement and extracorporeal
        digestion, their enzymes liquefying

dead tissue in wounds, and wonder,
        do I feed off the dead
who live inside me? When my mother was dying,
        she had a vision of her non-corporeal

father, brothers, sisters. Her last words,
        Why have you left me alone?

She never opened her eyes again,
        her chest a drowning well.

The bodily signs of death:
        the skin mottling as blood flow slows;
breathing, open mouthed; jaw, unhinged.
        I won't recount the signs of a dying marriage,

but he left two days after her funeral. Physically,
        he returned but told me he'd fallen
in love with someone else,
        that his love for me had passed.

Above my mother's body, orange mist
        had exhaled and dispersed, a light bulb
busted open, its luminescent gas escaping.
        The word fluorescent is so similar

to the word *florescence,* meaning flowering,
        and somewhere between these two,
there is a splendor I can barely stand.
        Inflorescence refers to flowers clustering

on one branch, each a separate floret,
        but if they are tightly clustered
as in the dandelion seed head, they look incomplete
        alone, though the whole is an illusion.

The word for this—*pseudanthium*—means "false
          flower." *Infrutescence*, its fruiting stage,
gives us grapes, ears of corn, stalks of wheat,
          so many of the berries we love.

This morning my hands ache
          as though in the night I'd been trying
to claw my way out of a hole
          I am down in, having lost the body

I came into this world through, and my husband's
          as well. It's almost as if my body
had come to believe his was a part of its own,
          a connection he would have to break or die.

Medical experts say it takes two moltings
          for maggots to do the job well,
to feed enough to clean a wound. I do not feel
          clean at all, though in our shower,

my husband and I still huddle some days,
          hunched into the spray. We call it *watering*.
When we do, we scrub each other, grateful
          for the living, dying flesh, but trying to get clean

of the other. Lately, he is more clear-eyed,

and it is as if a cicatrix husk is cracking.
Neither of us know who will emerge,

but he seems luminescent. I think that fawn

  he saved way back when we were new
in love must have had an identifying scar

  if it even lived after we released it
back into the wild where it belonged.

Saved from the Fall by Roy Batty

Brilliant minded, child
in emotions, overwhelmed by their moral
weight, in the end Roy Batty chose to save
Deckard, both men unlocked
then from the obligations of their lives.
In physics, when two particles meet,
even when separated, they are never
really apart, still effect the other,
what Einstein called
    spooky action at a distance.
I loved when Roy yanked Deckard up.
He could have let him fall.
Instead, he looked inward, became more
human than either of them had been
until then, recounting his memories:
    I've seen things you people wouldn't believe . . .
A gorgeous list—*shoulder of Orion; C-beams glittering*—
then actor Rutger Hauer, *being* Roy—ad libs,
    All those moments
    will be lost in time, like tears . . . in . . . rain.

What a strange love story, Batty and Deckard,
and the writer, director, actor, co-creators of Batty,
making me think of *sparticles*, superpartners
in physics, bosons and fermions, the way
relationship forms a kind of supersymmetry,

potential answer to why the fundamental forces
of the universe don't send us spinning
away from each other or collapsing inward,
    instead holding on,
hoping against
predictability.

Time is a Consequence

Relationship can be a confined space
in which people are pressed toward change.
In quantum mechanics, a particle escapes
bondage by *tunneling* behavior. All beings
are a mixture of both particle and wave—
     our genetics, histories, everything we
     experience, embedded memories,
     shared group attributes
(family, culture, gender, race, religion, class).
     Each love—
parent/child, lovers/spouses, siblings, even friends—
presses on us like geological force on a gem,
     and when we transition
(out of friendship, marriage, this life even?),
we move from individuality to collectivity,
and time is un-manifested. Scientists suggest
time is a consequence of our individuality,
our separateness part of the particle state,
the wave state the collective the future ·
emerges from, which I can believe, but can't
touch, and so want
     what I can hold
     in my hand
     against this cheek.

CODA

Dissimulation of Birds

After my spouse pulled away the last time, I saw the crows
on the roof of what had been our house weren't crows at all,
but a *murmuration* of starlings. Lipton's list on bird groups
pleases me,

A bouquet of pheasants | charm of finches | deceit of lapwings |
descent of woodpeckers | dole of doves |

      and though many birds flock,
only some fly densely—less then the space of one
body between them—as if a group soul choreographed
their dance, but that isn't true. An ornithologist
studying flocking behavior explains

exhalation of larks | fall of woodcocks | murder of crows |
ostentation of peacocks | parliament of owls |

      their undulating
lines, columns, spheres, and shifting planes aren't balletic,
not co-created delight, but evasive maneuvers,
compaction and decompaction, splitting and merging
      simply   a defense,
forming what are strangely named *terror waves,*

pitying of turtledoves | siege of herons | sord of mallards |
tidings of magpies | unkindness of ravens |

which pulse away
approaching predators. *Being single is always more risky,*
she writes. When my starlings—do they sense
danger in me?—leave my roof, they unfurl together,
    like fabric
    blocking the sky
and hover almost patiently, and I want to lift my arms,
let the wild night dress of them slip down over this body.